What Did You Do Yesterday?

Activity Book

T0352699

Name _____

Age _____

Class _____

OXFORD
UNIVERSITY PRESS

OXFORD
UNIVERSITY PRESS

Great Clarendon Street, Oxford OX2 6DP

Oxford University Press is a department of the University of Oxford.
It furthers the University's objective of excellence in research, scholarship,
and education by publishing worldwide in

Oxford New York

Auckland Bangkok Buenos Aires Cape Town Chennai
Dar es Salaam Delhi Hong Kong Istanbul Karachi Kolkata
Kuala Lumpur Madrid Melbourne Mexico City Mumbai
Nairobi São Paulo Shanghai Taipei Tokyo Toronto

OXFORD and OXFORD ENGLISH are registered trade marks of
Oxford University Press in the UK and in certain other countries

© Oxford University Press 2005

ISBN: 978 0 19 440161 6

Printed in China

Activities by: Christine Lindop
Illustrations by: Andy Hamilton
Original story by: Jacqueline Martin

Connect.

beach

doctor

lifeguard

nurse

slide

swimming
pool

train
station

Connect.

baseball •

card •

elephant •

hamburger •

lion •

monkey •

present •

sandcastle •

Circle yes or no .

❶ Mark's sister can swim. yes (no)

❷ Mark's father can swim. yes no

❸ The lifeguard had
red swimming shorts. yes no

❹ The lifeguard was in
the water. yes no

❺ Donna's mother went
to the hospital. yes no

❻ The doctor took an X-ray. yes no

❼ Donna hurt her right arm. yes no

❽ Donna hurt her arm
at the beach. yes no

❾ Donna sat on a bed. yes no

Number the sentences in order, 1 to 7.

☐ She saw the nurse.

☐ She went on the slide.

☐ The nurse took an X-ray of her arm.

1 Donna went to the park.

☐ Her mother took her to the hospital.

☐ Then she went home.

☐ She hurt her arm on the slide.

Circle the correct words.

1 Martin is Donna's
father (brother) uncle .

2 Martin went to the train station
supermarket swimming pool .

3 He met his Uncle David Andrew
Alan .

4 His uncle came by train car bicycle .

5 The train arrived at three four five
o'clock.

6 The train arrived at platform
one two three .

7 Uncle Alan had a
suitcase computer present .

8 Uncle Alan and Martin were
happy hungry tired .

Complete the sentences.

saw   went   ~~shops~~   baker's   T-shirt
green   shoes   bookstore   hand

❶ John went to the ___shops___ yesterday.

❷ He had a _____ T-shirt and brown _____.

❸ First he went to the _____.

❹ Then he _____ to the post office.

❺ The post office is next to the _____.

❻ He _____ his friend Steve.

❼ Steve had a letter in his _____.

❽ Steve had a white _____.

Where were they? Connect.

❶ Rachel went
to the zoo •

❷ They gave
the monkey •

❸ The monkey
was •

❹ The elephant
was •

❺ Kate and
Rachel •

❻ Maria went to •

❼ She took
home •

❽ There was
a computer •

• a banana.

• the library.

• with Kate.

• in a tree.

• on the desk.

• near the
water.

• five books.

• are friends.

Write the questions.

❶ Where did Tom and Rob go yesterday?
They went to the ball park.

❷ _____
They saw a baseball game.

❸ _____
Their caps were blue and white.

❹ _____
They ate hamburgers.

❺ _____
It was hot.

❻ _____
It was exciting.

❼ _____
Yes, they had fun.

Circle yes **or** no .

❶ Clare went to the baseball
game yesterday.   yes   (no)

❷ She was in bed all day.   yes   no

❸ Clare's pajamas were pink.   yes   no

❹ There were four comic books
on Clare's bed.   yes   no

❺ There was a box of tissues
on Clare's bed.   yes   no

❻ There was a purple elephant
on Clare's bed.   yes   no

❼ There was a brown monkey
on Clare's bed.   yes   no

❽ There were eight flowers
in the picture.   yes   no

❾ There was a lion on one
comic book.   yes   no

HAPPY
BIRTHDAY
9

Rearrange the words.

❶ went restaurant a Mike to yesterday
Mike went to a restaurant yesterday.

❷ family went he with his

_____

❸ his yesterday birthday was

_____

❹ was old he years nine

_____

❺ people were restaurant there at nine the

_____

❻ big Mike had cake a

_____

❼ lot he a presents of had

_____

❽ family him too his gave birthday cards

_____

❾ Mike happy was very

_____

Circle yes or no .

1 Amy went to the beach. (yes) no

2 Amy's grandparents
went to the office. yes no

3 Amy drank soda. yes no

4 Amy's grandparents
ate ice cream. yes no

5 They made sandcastles. yes no

6 Amy's mother went
to work at the hospital. yes no

7 Amy's father went
to the office. yes no

8 Amy's mother played
in the sea. yes no

9 Amy went to the hospital. yes no

1 **Complete the questions.**

What   Where   ~~Who~~   Where   What

❶ _____Who_____ did Martin meet?

❷ _____ did Kate and Rachel go?

❸ _____ did Maria take home?

❹ _____ was Clare yesterday?

❺ _____ did Amy make?

2 **Now number the answers.**

☐	They went to the zoo.
☐	She made sandcastles.
1	He met his Uncle Alan.
☐	She was in bed.
☐	She took home five books.

Complete the crossword.

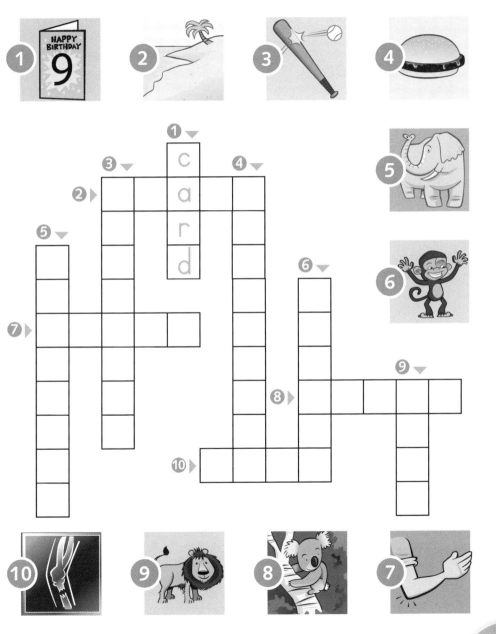

Where did they go? Connect.

❶ Mark went

❷ Donna went

❸ Martin went

❹ John went

❺ Kate and
Rachel went

❻ Maria went

❼ Tom and
Rob went

❽ Mike went

❾ Amy went

❿ Amy's father went

• to the zoo.

• to the train station.

• to the office.

• to a restaurant.

• to the hospital.

• to the library.

• to the swimming pool.

• to the beach.

• to the ball park.

• to the shops.